NO ONE WILL EVER BELIEVE YOU

Poems about Bill Murray

Shea Stripling

ISBN-13: 9780996746540
ISBN-10: 0996746544

Hypertrophic Press
P.O. Box 423, New Market, AL, 35761
www.hypertrophicpress.com

Book design: Jeremy Bronaugh
Cover design: Jeremy Bronaugh

For Bill
& Bob Harris
& Herman Blume
& Phil Connors
& Frank Cross
& Larry Darrell
& a few other people I've left
spectacularly sentimental voicemails

contents

I definitely need a long, slow root canal.

35

That was quite an outfit you weren't wearing earlier.

36

Best day ever, greatest day of my life.

39

I know I can't hear you, but I know I can pick up what
you're saying, baby.

40

Love me, feed me, never leave me.

42

You work, you get paid, you drink.

44

We are oft to blame in this, 'tis too much proved that with
devotions pious we do sugar o'er the devil himself.

46

This isn't the old Mister Sunshine.

48

Everybody wants to launch a rocket.

49

Take a cigarette.

51

Thanks so much for coming to my Christmas special.

52

You go on ahead.

54

Do I have any volunteers?

56

So I got that goin' for me, which is nice.

58

This is an elephant graveyard of faces you cannot name.

61

That's my train.

62

The expeditor of your dreams, pal.

Untangling my affinity for Bill Murray is a bit like trying to unravel the rubber band and paperclip masses you find while feeling around for a pair of scissors. The beginnings are knotted in an indecipherable mass of late night television programming and in-flight entertainment where *Groundhog Day* or *Stripes* or *Caddyshack* is playing in loop.

The clearest moment I can recall is when I was sitting in the red glow of Christmas flipping aimlessly back and forth until I settled on that scene in *Groundhog Day* where Bill is dancing with Andie MacDowell in the snow. They're waltzing under this pavilion covered in lights and he dips her over the side, her brown curls spilling over the railing. That great Ray Charles song "You Don't Know Me" is twinkling in the background, and he pulls her close and puts her hand on his heart. You're waiting for a kiss that never comes.

The moment hangs like a drip on an icicle.

Expectant.

Inevitable.

I stayed up long enough to see TBS's second showing.

Afterward, I lay in bed feeling important. My ceiling was dotted with those plastic glow-in-the-dark stars. I stared at them with my near-sighted stare until the stars and the feelings were a blur.

That scene is called "French Poetry" because just before the dance Rita reveals over dinner with Phil that her undergraduate self studied 19th-century French poetry. It struck my undergraduate self while reading Donald Revell's translation of Rimbaud's *The Illumina-*

tions that "Winter Festival" is just the sort of poem that Rita would read to Phil in their queen-sized bed stuffed with down pillows, thinking of that dance in February. And Phil would listen until she was finished, tuck one of her curls behind her ear, place his lips just moments from hers, and say, "What a waste of time."

NO ONE WILL EVER BELIEVE YOU

You like boats but not the ocean.

He waltzes in: Can I buy you a drink?
Sweet vermouth on the rocks with a twist, please.
There's something so familiar here, I think.

You give your hand to me and then we sink.
The snow starts in on us, the hardest freeze.
He waltzes in: Can I buy you a drink?

He wakes up, the bedside roses of pink.
Radio plays the "I got you babe" tease.
There's something so familiar here, I think.

The groundhog bestows on the crowd a wink.
Phil looks to the camera with his unease.
He waltzes in: Can I buy you a drink?

Her rhinestones and French poetry in ink
like a subtle paint-by-numbers striptease.
There's something so familiar here, I think.

There's no tomorrow today: doublethink.
He waltzes in: Can I buy you a drink?
There's something so familiar here, I think.

I wish I had a theatre that was only open when it rained.

The smell of the air was fat,
swollen, a sitcom pregnancy
holding the bottom of a cloud
bulge waddling toward a plate of pickles
and peanut butter,
threatening to break water over the downtown area.

And we waited for it like expectant sitcom fathers
flicking cigarettes out the open window,
pacing back and forth,
scripts in hand.

He suggests we start rehearsing the climax,
the scene that everyone will be talking about
after they've witnessed "Return to the Love Canal,"
the one that will leave them saying:
"What happened?"

A boom from within the cloud bulge from stage left:
Braxton Hiccups.

"Let's start from
'This marriage is a cesspool we should have abandoned
in the 70s.'"
I say the line and cross the room
to complete my action
(cutting a tomato into slices
that represent my subconscious desire
to do something obvious).

And then the clouds rupture,
water breaking on the treetops
and sidewalks
and the old women's plastic rain bonnets.

She smokes.

I built her a bookshelf.
Made a space by the bathtub,
carved a square in the ceramic tile,
collected the cotton candy insulation,
relocated rat families,
sanded boards with my stubble,
stained the oak with sherry,
placed her plays spine to spine,
filled the empty spots with stories.

She turned off the TV with her toe.
The Tahitian teal of the nail,
the graying gray of the dial,
the wedding white of the tub,
the worn wood of the finger,
the rust red of the radiator,
the scrubby cream of the tiles,
the blue blue of her eyes,
the wet yellow of her hair.

She comes in colors
by way of the green line bus.
You get it.

I find her in the Serengeti
area of the Natural History Museum.
The taxidermied lions frozen mid-feast
stare in awkward glass-eyed silence
as we pull out the sleeping bags
and commence taking sad songs, making them better.

The best summer camp experience available in this price range.

Are you ready for the summer?

This summer I'm looking for some action. Let's you and me press ourselves processed-cheese-like between bunk beds in the counselors' cabin. I'll remove your Hawaiian shirt button-by-button with the precision of an indoor climber moving up those multicolored plastic nodules. It's Sexual Awareness Week at camp, and I've got a full thermos of coffee and a wad of candy-colored condoms. You can keep my polka-dotted panties, run them up the flagpole at half-mast if necessary.

Are you ready for the summer?

I hoist the yellow canoe into the trailer and pull the sleeves of the Alf sweatshirt tight around the waist of my purple one-piece: standard summer camp issue. You open the bus door with your knee and slap Alf's snout hanging limp on half of my ass before the singing starts.

Are you ready for the summer?

And we're here. I do all the paddling: a plodding chop-stick in this ramen soup river pushing toward the back of your boyish good lucks. You are in repose with ukulele accompaniment, a butterfly pinned to your lifejacket.

Are you ready for the summer?

We dock the banana boat on a mound of mud, our sneakers stuck in halfway. We scamper and slip into the bushes leaving our Grauman's Chinese Theatre imprints behind us. And there are the blueberries. I pick and you spectate, catching the occasional berry that makes its way to the ground and then pitching it up toward the crevice between my breasts. Bullseye.

Are you ready for the summer?

The Paramount mountain is surrounded by stars. Somewhere beneath that starlight is the line of clothes scattered en route to the skinny dipping scene, which always reminded me a bit of the rapture: empty clothes abandoned by the ascended. Then in the black water, feet steadied by water moccasins, the long lake water kiss before some more comic relief and a fight to get to the beach where the panties have already been raided and run up every flagpole in a five-mile radius.

The second verse same as the first, a little bit louder and a little bit worse.

And it ends with the stamping out of the last campfire and a marshmallow whimper.

Chicks dig me because I rarely wear underwear (and when I do it's usually something unusual).

I WANT YOU.

YES, YOU IN THE AMERICAN FLAG BRIEFS
(I ASSUME).

I say this to the pixels, and as I do a little beer spittle flies from my lip to twinkle your laptop eye. I wipe and destroy a little world that I don't fully understand where maybe a pixel gal was trying to woo a pixel guy. Stripes of color on stripes of color. A 3D stereogram poster. I hold my eyes on stalks up to the screen and squint. Clint Eastwood in a summer sandstorm. And there it is, the full picture:

I'm sitting on the griddle, legs agape in olive green. Your hand on the ice cream scoop and a smile on your face. We're kissing and kissing and kissing 'til kissing is just talking and crossing lips like legs.

It's cute because we're going nowhere.

I hate to advocate drugs, liquor, violence, and insanity to anyone, but in my case it's worked.

In the beginning there was a Bloody Mary,
Tabasco and tomato replaced the sun
surrounded by the shit left over from the crawfish boil,
huevos rancheros forcefully forced from muskets
into the muzzles of Hell's Angels.

And in the beginning there was Wild Turkey
coiled rattlesnake copper in an afternoon IV,
helpful snakebites on each vein,
side-by-side staple remover
exit wounds.

And in the beginning there was instant coffee,
voluntary insomnia leading us into the unknown
known of post-3am: a burbling feeling in the pits
of stomachs not unlike the bottom of the coffee pot
murmurs of that demented DEADLINE DEADLINE
DEADLINE.

And in the beginning there were Dunhill cigarettes
hanging loose from the mouth of a Nixon mask
hanging loose on the head of a stuffed bat
poised over the typewriter in the moving car,
loose lit ends singeing the paper edges.

And in the beginning there was Chartreuse with ginger,
lime green light strained through a casino visor onto
pickled pink eyeballs bounding from number to number
roulette wheel style: black, red, black, red,
Bust.

And in the beginning there was Halcyon,
Benzos for Bozos, blue kingfishers,
a lucky break, a bright blue interval set in the midst
of adversity, a lull in the instant coffee insomnia,
a break in the clouds for bird brains.

"And in the end, the times you ache
are equal to the times you fake,"
said the man as he was packed
into the cannon with the same
hands he used to pack his pipe.

And it was good.

Holy Christ, what am I lookin' at?

Looking through the binoculars
toward the end of summer
I saw the lighthouse.
You could run down the Esplanade
mouth 'morning' at dogs
and women in stirrup pants
to reach it.
It's a bed and breakfast,
that lighthouse.
I can just make out
the rose on a white tray with
the most eligible bagel.
Last night, I drank down the remainder
of wine in the fridge door,
held the binoculars up with one hand,
and moved the needle over two grooves:
Le temps de l'amour.

She's my Rushmore.

You punctuate your phrases with sips,
the cheap wine commas.
Negative air, negative time filled
with the humming of conversations
and the silence between our silverware.
You wrap the paper straw holder around the glass.
After dinner you wipe your mouth and say thank you
just like this:
"I need to go to the bathroom."

Last night you waited until I was asleep to slip out
of my arms and into a bath.
I heard you turn the water on and off
with your pruning foot,
the squeak of the pipes as they quenched and released,
a conversation begun and aborted.
I smoothed down the fibers of my moustache
with my index finger
and considered the indention in your feather pillow.
It should be bronzed.
It should be set on someone's mantel
like those baby shoes that no one seems to save
anymore.

Now, I look at your blue sweater hanging
on the back of your empty chair
like a scarecrow.
Scarecrows have become so happy and useless.
I am so happy and so useless.

You haven't come back from the bathroom,
so I write this thing down in crayon
on the paper tablecloth.

I'm a bit lonely these days.

**But what they don't tell you is you never forget
an elephant.**

Sometimes the circus comes to town.
You put on your red and white overalls.
You ask someone to pigtail your hair.
That someone (tall) drives you
to the Foodland parking lot.
The elephant is a lady.
She stands beside a trailer full of half-priced pork chops.
There is fresh chicken manure in the field
across the street.
You sit on her top.
You touch her wire hairs.
You feel like "The Blue Danube" waltz.

Please don't call me by my real name. It destroys the reality I'm trying to create.

I had missed the discotheque. Every train that pulled to the subway platform was brimming with people and their sweat. I had tried twice to wedge myself shoulder-first into the compartment only to have the doors clamp shut prematurely. By the time a semi-empty train arrived it was ten minutes past seven, and I knew my party was already sliding down the opposite tunnel in their leather boots and body glitter.

The city was drowsy when I emerged from the tunnel. A smattering of streetlights shone intermittently on the slick street. The night was shot; there was a time slot to be filled.

Three choices presented themselves at the convenience store: red, white, or sparkling. Obviously there wasn't a wrong choice, so I selected the sparkling (a dessert wine) and a dessert (some Italian equivalent of the Ding Dong). I left with my paper bag and a bit of optimism.

Sweet vermouth on the rocks with a twist would have been more appropriate because, as Phil Connors points out, it reminds one of "Rome, the way the sun hits the buildings in the afternoon." Yet, the convenience store wine (drunk straight from the bottle because our room had only empty kitchen cabinets) went down smoothly after the initial shock of popping the cork. I enjoyed the bottle sip by sip in the deep hotel bathtub situated below an impending hot water heater.

Before departing from the States, I had checked out a copy of W. Somerset Maugham's *The Razor's Edge*. I began the book in the bath and couldn't stop until the bottle was empty and the water was cold.

I definitely need a long, slow root canal.

The tongue was a stage, the teeth tiny seats. Guests would sink into their tiny teeth seats and watch orange slices in sequined tights perform the Pechanga atop the pink platform.

Lovely tongue-lashing
Lip to lip to licorice
Holding ice on tongue

Hold me in your mouth like a puppy with sealed eyes. Cradle me in your lazy lockjaw. Carry me to the room, each inch an enjambment.

Hungry hungry hip
O's of the moon and sun full
Plate-lickers delight

I have a habit of picking things up and putting them in my mouth. Piaget said the oral phase was over for me, but I find my empty mouth lacking. The tongue is a lonely hunter.

Lips on leather eggs
A pickled dogwood flower
Kleptomania

That was quite an outfit you weren't wearing earlier.

And that was it.
I want to kiss you silly, and we'll sleep better after,
so he pressed his pretty pleats
to the collision of my collarbone.
Is that ok?
Yes, but please, sir, I'd like some more.
And there were more.
The tongues like children
encountering a revolving door.
The things you see when you
(this *you* being me and not you)
open your eyes:
pink stationery, pencil shavings, broken flowers
on the hardwood floor.
When you sleep in someone else's bed
you dream differently.
The smell of strange laundry detergent,
the off-kilter alignment of the headboard
gets into your head.

And you
(actually *I*)
try to focus on the rhythm of your tongue,
the placement of your hands,
but when you waste the day in the produce aisle,
artichoke hearts aren't easily dismissed.
My mind is back to earlier this evening
when we were surrounded by potato chips
and packaged bologna,
the spot where you lost all your celebrity.
In the grocery store, you're just a guy pushing my cart.

Yet, you are Bill Murray, so you make eyes at me
when I put Chicken in a Biscuit in the cart
and sample the samples.

You're sort of the worst sometimes,
like when I mispronounce *baguette* and *brioche*.
Or when I pretend to cough and insert yet-to-be-
purchased grapes in my mouth.
And yet
I want to run my hands through your receding hairline.
I want to kiss you under the vegetable misters
as peals of fake thunder crash in the background.
I want you to place one hand on the small of my back
as I examine avocados that will inevitably go soft
before guacamole can be made.

The produce aisle always brings out this side of me.
Everything is ripening, rounding.
People are sniffing, squeezing.
It's a cliché, but this doesn't make it less true.

Which brings us back to those artichoke hearts.
Do we
(yes, this time it's you and me buried in a box spring)
pull them from artichoke bodies like those red-cheeked
natives in *Temple of Doom*?
If one is a vegetarian
(and this one is),
does this mean this one's heart
can only be an artichoke heart,
which bristles purple at the sound of coffee dripping

and Karen Carpenter?
Broccoli blooms greener with steaming, so it stands to
reason your innards are unripening,
returning to vines, vermillion, don't you think?
You're browning in my bated breath,
edges curling rather than crisping.
Let's get back in our drawers.

Best day ever, greatest day of my life.

We were sea otters:
cracking clam hearts
on hard rock bellies
over
and
over
and
over,
muscles overworked,
moanings overwrought
until a snap,
a rock candy crackle,
broken wide:
a pearly denouement.

I know I can't hear you, but I know I can pick up what you're saying, baby.

LIVE ON AIR.
From red to gray with a flick.
Bill Murray the K ate the remaining half
of a glazed donut
with the last of the cold coffee grounds:
black gravel scooped from the bottom of a fish tank
with a tiny green net.
He thought of something off the cuff,
wrote it on the unbrowned edge of the napkin.

I flicked from station to station
waiting for the used car commercial to conclude
so we could be reunited in the air.
I ate a cherry popsicle that threatened to drip
on the white leather interior,
made two laps on the radio station spectrum before
taking to the hot streets in high heels
and cat-eye glasses.

Smoke gets in your eyes
when you're running around idling cars,
and when you do aerobic exercise
sweat gets in your eyes.
I'm dancing up Broadway on the piano keys of
Del Shannon's "Runaway"
when I see him.

He's in the studio
sucking on his own cherry popsicle,
feet propped up on the sound board.
Our eyes meet through the glass.

Sans popsicle,
he starts moving his mouth.
He spoke to me.
He spoke to me right through the window.
I think he said *I love you.*

Love me, feed me, never leave me.

Ingredients:

2 cups of flour: He has it on his nose, his lips, his hair.
A regular cocaine snowman. You could cut out
star-shaped sugar cookies on his stomach.

3 eggs: He cracks them all in one swift stroke of his fist.
The shells and whites and yolks are indistinguishable.
Someone might think a live birth had taken place.

1 cup of sugar: He licks it off of a stick of butter. The
white crystals glisten on his rubbery tongue as it hangs
out of his head like a prize ribbon.

2 tsp. vanilla: He pours it on his chest in a biblical way.
The dark liquor drips from the tiny black ringlets. There
are brown dots on my toes.

*½ tsp. salt: He knocks over the shaker with his foot as
he mounts the table. The place settings are in disarray.
Our name cards are not side by side.

*¼ tsp. yellow food coloring: He has it on his fingertips.
A slow yellow fever contraction.

Directions:

1. Preheat the oven: He kisses my earlobes and rubs the skin behind my knees where I rarely shave.

2. Stir the ingredients to homogeneity: Our lips (mine covered in chocolate and coconut shavings, his in melted butter and red sprinkles) meet.

3. Pour into the pan: He carries me to the bed with Garfield sheets.

4. Bake: I close my eyes and try to keep up.

5. Remove from the oven and allow time to cool: Each of us naked, breathing deeply, him smoking a candy cane.

You work, you get paid, you drink.

He mowed the dirt patch in an undershirt.
The radio said
"Come in, I'll give you shelter from the storm."
And so he came in complaining of the heat,
sat down on the toilet seat and started on another job.
He held the crescent between his thumb and forefinger,
one foot on the toilet like George Washington
crossing the room to cup her breasts.
The way he weighed the cantaloupes
in the supermarket, biting his bottom lip.
Her fingertips covered in dried glue
he peeled away until
he had a spare pair of hands to hold.
He did errands and she took baths in his tub
listening to the bats swaying in the ceiling
and removed dead cockroaches with old newspapers.
The old newspaper building was demolished
on the fourth of July,
all the dust in their hair fell to the floor
making a Pompeii of the bath mat.
In the morning she stood at the window
in striped panties.
He called her his little chimney bird
and the neighbor flicked open his blinds to see them
sitting on cushions sipping vodka tonics and
sinking battleships and sweating in sleep
and salivating on pillow cases
and spilling onto sidewalks lined with poppies
dreaming of puppies they would hold
on patent leather leashes and parade
in front of those women

in their floral pedal pushers and push-up bras.
They drank cider and waltzed on fingertips
in front of the bay window,
buttocks rounded plum peach persimmon he called
a perfectly good ass,
the dead Black-Eyed Susans
in the blackest moss of the plastic pot
where the other woman had grown her tomatoes,
the mornings thick with steam
and her raspberry tea turning all the cups pink.

We are oft to blame in this, 'tis too much proved that with devotions pious we do sugar o'er the devil himself.

I broke in through this window once.

This was after they turned her house into a book bindery, but before someone spray-painted Bill Murray's white silhouette on the door. I was wearing a corsage and a blue dress with all the frills. It must have been an Indian summer because by the end of the night my hair was curly and his was straight. We spent most of the night in a gym covered in crepe paper with hands slightly above hips and shoulder blades. I was waiting for the floor to turn into a swimming pool; he was waiting for me to fall in.

Each time I spoke he would run his index finger along the length of his sparse moustache and inhale slowly like this: -------->

It was at this point that I remembered my grandmother. If it's important for you to picture her, think Joan Crawford wearing a pink housecoat with brown flowers, holding a one-eyed tabby.

"It's the corner down there," she said and threw a piece of bologna on the floor for the tabby. "That's where Bill Murray saw me mowing the grass in my two-piece. It was a riot. Bill Murray was a preacher, and I was the baby Jesus. I was standing there wiping sweat off the tops of my breasts when he drove into a fire hydrant."

Back in the present, I told my date I was ready to go, but he insisted I stay and step on his feet some more. We got in the car. I rolled down the window and let in the smell of fresh fertilizer. Gladys and the Pips came on the radio and, like clockwork, he proceeded to run his hand up and down my thigh under the guise of searching for gum. I unhooked my seatbelt and rolled to the curb.

This was the place.

I staggered from the road to this grass and this pavement. This was where she reached for a star.

I picked up a piece of crumbled asphalt and tossed it at the lowest window. I crawled in through the cracks, which took a fair chunk of my tulle with them. I sat on the cold concrete next to a stack of clothbound books with titles written in white out.

I unpaused her story.

"He whistled and then he rode into the sunset, tale as old as time. My daddy died, so the house was mine. I filled it with dirty laundry and bad habits. I found a man who filled my good wine glasses with dip and hid Foodland cashiers in my lingerie. It's hard to swap stardust for flesh. All I asked was that he be true, be true, be true."

This isn't the old Mister Sunshine.

Because I've never been to Paris,
I imagine him in the most stereotypical
of French situations:

Bill Murray walking down a cobblestone path,
Bill Murray drinking coffee from a porcelain cup,
Bill Murray carrying flowers wrapped in brown paper,
Bill Murray pretending to like the wine,
Bill Murray pretending to like the accordion,
Bill Murray wearing a red scarf,
Bill Murray being surprised at how long you have to
      chew a slice of baguette,
Bill Murray reflected in a puddle of moonlight,
Bill Murray comparing his head to a block of cheese,
Bill Murray feeling the fabric of a beret,
Bill Murray tentatively wearing a beret,
Bill Murray feeling bolder about the beret after
      a glass of Champagne,
Bill Murray feeling overwhelmed
      with an unspeakable awe,
Bill Murray feeling aimless desire,
Bill Murray touching the petals of the table roses,
Bill Murray ending a postcard with 'love&love&love.'

Everybody wants to launch a rocket.

I walk the dog up the hill where the trees are cleared for the power lines.

The Saturn V stands erect at 6am just like the good and decent Americans in their full-size beds. It's a replica, that rocket. The original had to be laid to rest in a horizontal position because of a half-remembered fact about an agreement with Russia someone at Space Camp explained to me while I ate Dippin' Dots (the Ice Cream of the Future) from a plastic pouch.

At night I drive by and see Bill Murray astride the plaster fuselage, thighs squeezing propellants into submission, one hand held aloft: Slim Pickens in *Dr. Strangelove* meets John Travolta in *Urban Cowboy*. I see him touch the night sky with that same hand, a sky someone might compare to velvet, but I'm thinking suede as the space texture changes with his touch.

Bill bounces down a shifting Lite Brite hallway and lands on the Jupiter spot. Paul Shaffer plays the monolith piano while Bill sings "Star Wars, nothing but, Star Wars, give me those Star Wars, don't let them end." And the curtain closes on atom bomb crashes like Christmas bulbs breaking on hardwood floors.

You're the villain, I guess, but you're still the most likeable person in this movie.

Take a cigarette.
after The Song Of The Lark by Jules Breton

Art
like Bill Murray
is an idea
I like to pursue
when I'm alone.

Just sit on the bench with that painting for a bit.
Art museums are so quiet.
Art is so quiet.
She's so quiet.

So I stay sitting with her on the bench
barefoot on the miles to nowhere,
her worn bamboo stick feet.
She's walked the wrong direction.
Not just the wrong direction
in terms of where she lives
but the wrong direction
in terms of
wanting to stay alive.

But there's something beyond that, too.
Something fuzzy,
a yolk on her horizon
she could scramble and serve with that sickle.

And I look,
and I don't want to go.
And I hear the song,
the lark,
and I decide you won't.

Thanks so much for coming to my Christmas special.

I took the village down from the attic today,
set up the miniature Phils
(Connors and Punxsutawney)
next to the porcelain Carl Spackler and gopher.
And this year I made the bold choice to put Garfield
between the tiny "Don't Hassle Me, I'm Local" T-shirt
and tiny headless Chevy Chase.

Baby steps through the living room.
Baby steps to the kitchen.

You're taller than me so you put the star
on top of the Grand Budapest Hotel
while I decorate the *Ghostbusters II* cookies
(it was the original cast, but SOMEONE
ate the Mr. Stay Puft marshmallow, so there's that).
Also, I don't know if you noticed when you came in,
but I got that animatronic scene
from *Hyde Park on Hudson*
where FDR gets a very tasteful handjob in a Buick
to light up.

Baby steps to the window.

God, I love this time of year
when everyone puts out their *Space Jam* nativity
and sings "Ghostbusters" by the fire.
Did you see they painted the opening scene
from *Lost in Translation*
on the windows at Foodland?
You know, that tight shot of Scarlett Johansson's ass

in sheer pink panties
with 'Lost in Translation' written across it?
It's gorgeous!
This year I want to drive around and take pictures of
all the snowmen dressed like Nick the Lounge Singer
and Osmosis Jones,
paste them in a scrapbook with Steve Zissou stickers.

I'm beat.
Let's say we lie down in all this torn wrapping paper
and drink Suntory whisky until we get good
and relaxed,
then I'll fold back your Ernie McCracken comb-over
for a kiss
and give you that set of knives I've been hiding
in the hall closet.

You go on ahead.

Boot heels kick back volcanic sand
unveiling layers of treasure:
broken BIC lighters, bits of tin foil
snatched up by magpie fingers lusty for the shiny,
the glint of an eye,
the jingle-jangling light of a silver key ring
reverberating,
the magpie scraping together bits
for his slick nest of ceramic tiles and window panes
to lick and stick in rows of relics
of other walks down other beaches.

Bombay Sapphire in those Lunartinis still sparkling
behind these pairs of morning eyes,
facets reflecting the fumbling of hands
on glasses like the fingers of lunar tides
on moon beaches,
the space laughter, the chatter of space gulls,
the silence of the silent space hula reverberating
beneath the Eddie Fisher serenade
on a Port Authority bus bound for moon sand.
And now they boarded that same bus again
with the little tickets of foil,
sat down in seats and waited to return to NYC
and all of the gravity
and pavement pain.

The space food, once taken from the space oven,
removed from the space foil,
was placed on the blue space plates
with sweet space chutney,

the smell reverberating
in the nest of ceramic tiles and window panes,
littered with the relics of space beaches.
The magpie and the girl sat side-by-side
facing the blueberry Earth behind the window pane
holding freeze-dried potatoes in their mouths
and the space blueberry in their eyes.
They did their best to empty their heads
of all the space sand.

The foil-thin plastic of the bus window panes
separating the breath of space from the eye,
but not the resounding of memory
stuck in the corners like sand.

Do I have any volunteers?

A touch of my finger
a brush
revealing a bit of your unexposed backbone.

Bones buried in flesh.

You're so many structures strung together in this solid
sediment shifted and sifted from year to year
until you settled.

The time of us is shrinking.

Cardboard boxes full of us
packed and sent to the curator,
smudgy letters and pressed flowers
pinned behind plate glass,
our bedroom reproduced
with wax figurines and halogen lighting.

Children boarding school buses to see our jelly jars
full of coins,
groups with brochures watching the video of our last
day play in loop.
A kiss on the head and a wave of the hand.

My hand looks so small next to yours.
"Expansion, Explosion, Expulsion," says the marker
below our bed where the waxy you holds my waxy
cheek to your waxy chest.

A boy buys a tiny you
and a tiny me
from the gift shop
and pretends we're not extinct.

So I got that goin' for me, which is nice.

Let the clubbing of chubby flower tops begin.

Red.
Yellow.
Orange.
Fore.

Knock the sunset back to the back 40.

The Dalai Lama takes a good slice off the top.
Something you can really sink your teeth into:
Baby Ruth nougat.

Follow it with one eye until it sinks into the crook
of a turf hip,
a real sinking feeling
accompanied by that hollow rattle.

"He's gotta be happy with that,"
the announcers murmur,
as reliable as a religious chant.

Lama takes his yellow-tinted glasses off,
rubs the bridge of his nose,
turns up the radio on the golf bag:

Chime.
Chime.
Chime.

Chant.
Chant.
Chant.

His throat singing
like an engine trying to turn over
spooks the others' shots.

At the 18th hole the Dalai Lama takes a mulligan,
pulls his flower from the rough,
tosses it overhanded
while the monks aren't watching.

This is an elephant graveyard of faces you cannot name.

He held his hands one-by-one over the driver side air vent and became a bowler cooling fingers waiting for his ball to be disgorged from the mouth of the return. After another 45 minutes of construction traffic, he approached his limit.

Exit 168 was promising. The series of blue signs portioned out the great indispensables of life into three distinct categories: Fuel; Lodging; Food. He was in the market for the latter. The Food category here was helpfully subdivided: Tex-Mex, Pizza, Seafood, and the vague "American." He washed up at Captain D's.

The wooden interior was painted a Cape Cod white and had pockets of carpenter ant erosion around the windows. At the counter, the cashier was wearing a lime green polo and the listless look listed as an occupational hazard of service in the fast food industry. The little slice of the sea in the middle of suburban sprawl smelled of nameless homogenous fish and vinegar. It was the vinegar that had reeled Bill in; Captain D was the only titan of the American fast food industry who dared to name vinegar as a condiment.

At the condiment station, he gathered the plastic malt bottle and two paper cups full of ketchup. At his booth, Bill delicately dripped two drops of vinegar into each paper well and sprinkled pepper in their wake. The whole concoction was then mixed to homogeneity with a plastic fork. At this point, the cashier brought his beige tray of fish and sides to his table.

"Thank you."

"My pleasure," she said in a way that let him know it wasn't.

That's my train.

That suitcase was full of
tandoori chicken
saag paneer
shrimp pakora
a semi-venomous snake
potato samosas
tamarind chutney
sweet lime
a leather belt with my initials
onion bhaji
a Hotel Chevalier robe (on loan)
mase
a Kinks record
my feather

and I left it on top of the damn sleeper car.

Valentine's Day. Bummer.

Valentine's Day 2016.
The bingo cage turns on Peter Venkman's command,
the clatter of the conversation hearts on the metal ribs:
the dull rattle of a cicada husk in a water bottle.
He plunges his hand into the pastel jumble,
pulls a pale pink heart out in one fist,
holds it to his temple.
"I'm going to go out on a limb and say it's BE MINE,
BE MINE."
He brings the closed hand down,
opens it.
"Right again.
That should impress some of the ladies in the room."
Blue hairs adjust their reading glasses,
move conversation hearts over bingo cards.
A man in the back dislodges a piece of
ectoplasm from the back of his throat in one foul hack.
"Apocalypse now.
Please."

I wonder if it remembers me.

I lie back in the water and listen to my very own breathing. The laptop is sitting atop the seat of the toilet, which is adjacent to the tub. I watch your lips open and close and know you are saying words that mean: something.

I am in the water. You are in the water. We are, for all intents and purposes, in the same water.

Early on, I learned the water in my mug, my aquarium, and my plastic swimming pool was the same water in ancient man's hand, ditch, and hole. I learned water can travel through time, through bodies. It can be in icebergs or clouds or puddles or wine or mayonnaise or saliva or sex or birth or mud or udders or Champagne bubbles or rocket fuel or breast milk or melted cheese or ink blots or egg yolks or lip gloss or placenta or paella or the ocean you currently inhabit.

This water cradling the curve of my hip could have touched your lips or hips or any number of body parts. It could have carried you to the surface for a breath and bobbed you on top of itself. This water beaded on your body suit, in your beard, could have vaporized in the air and drifted for miles until raining on this city, running down these drains, and pouring through these pipes on top of me.

Watching you, I think of how words spoken under water turn into bubbles, the sound sealed up in the sea. Your lines leave your lips, and you swear they're spoken by the character Steve Zissou. But your mouth, your lips, your hips don't know the difference. There's no filter. The words roll off your tongue and into the ocean with the ease of skin divers.

I'm the king of the cul-de-sac.

Bill Murray doesn't have a star on the Walk of Fame.

I checked.

I spent the better part of four hours walking through a never-ending loop of hookah bars and exotic wig shops and was forced to seek shelter in "New York's Finest Pizza." Forced to eat the last slice of day-old pepperoni still lying under the heat bulb. Forced to share a booth with a guy named Johnny. Forced to hear all about that time Johnny stayed in the same hotel as Sylvester Stallone. Forced to explain who Bill Murray was to a gift shop cashier who replied "That guy that pulled the shit out of the pool in *Caddyshack*? He doesn't have a star."

I wanted to feel like those tourists who make pilgrimages to the Via Dolorosa. I wanted to walk with a caravan of disciples dressed as Carl Spackler and Peter Venkman through the streets lined with peddlers pushing plastic Phil Connors into my hands. I wanted to stop at each station where Bill "Tied His Shoe," "Made a Sarcastic Comment," or "Encountered a Pigeon" and imagine myself walking beside him. I wanted to place a package of golf balls and a tumbler of Suntory whisky on the hallowed ground.

And yet. And yet.

Bill's steps are untraceable. There are whisperings of SoHo restaurants where he pilfered French fries off of a couple's plate, Chicago bars where he poured unwanted glasses of Scotch for Cubs fans, and Canadian karaoke bars where he sang Elvis to coeds. But there is no definitive guide.

Who wants popcorn?

I wore a thrift store floral with one broken strap.
Paper doll paisley.
It fit the theme.
Sixties. Pastel. Summer.
I look at the picture from that night
and see a happy sunburn on a fat face,
a sunburn standing in front of a glossy movie poster.
A glossy movie poster that now hangs
above my green couch.

That night I bought a paper bag of popcorn
that my seat partner declined.
That seat partner being that poster.
I waited at the box office for them to roll him up,
cinch his waist with a rubber band
and hand him over to my buttered hands.

I had a g&t at my feet
because it was that kind of theatre,
and I accidentally sent it spilling to the front row
when Bill came on the screen
because I'm that kind of girl.
It was *Moonrise Kingdom.*
It was my first time seeing Bill on screen after
arrivederci.

The movie made you feel like you were
full of possibility and French.
Interesting beyond reason.
In love enough to order dessert.
In need of a small cup of coffee,

a mustard-colored sweater,
and a someone on the other end of a telephone.

It was over,
and I was walking under connect-the-dot streetlights.
He could probably hear the cicadas
and the slur of whimsy on the voicemail.
I like to think he listened to it
and then opened a window.

How many angels can dance on the head of a pin?

This coin is suspended
in the thick of May,
the humidity holding
it still within itself.

The face on the coin
squints in the light
along with the assembled
crowds gathered to see the spectacle,
water shooting from a ceramic conch shell
pressed to the mouth of a Poseidon type.

Backs of various builds —
flat cutting boards,
collapsed flour bags,
cottage cheese —
turned toward the spray
tossing coins over shoulders.
Like water.
Like nothing.

The wishes are caught there:
stuck in suspended animation.
The atmosphere,
thick as curls of gelato,
full of expectation.

My hand is open.
This wish is swinging on a pendulum.
Between
true.

Between
false.

You're supposed to wish for
a second-helping of Rome,
but the promise of summer —
summer vacation,
summer romance,
summer reinvention —
emboldens you
to stretch out your fingers
just a bit farther.
I turn the coin over in my hand,
in my mind,
in the hand
in my mind,
and retell
the story to myself
of who I paid a cent
to see.

You wanna have a funeral party while you're alive so you can go?

A powdered sugar apparition appeared
over the Mississippi.
It blew in on a southerly
and formed a face over the surface of the waters.
The rolling blunder of horns and cymbals joined in,
injected itself into Hurricanes and test tube shots,
dusted the entertainment district stench —
an open mouth that's recently contained beer
and hush puppies —
with a Cafe du Monde tin full of ashes —
presumably Bill Murray's.
But as the neon flyer flock flapped down Bourbon Street
advertising clowns and nude women,
behind the brass band playing "Ghostbusters"
one could just barely make out a man in dark glasses
turning to Jon Favreau,
telling him to get
a theme song.

I make it a rule never to get involved with possessed people.

The laptop leaves a warm space where a body
could have been.
You're muted.
I watch your lips form words
I heard once while sitting atop a pile
of unpaired socks.

Then, I dip my sour apple Blow Pop
into a can of Coke
every time you get slimed.

Now I wonder
how you interacted with a green screen.
The screen
that represented
a ghost
that represented
a man
(so says the DVD commentary).

How did you act when no one reacted?
You had to fill in the lines
in your mind
for a counterpart
that ceased to exist.

I imagine you carried the screen to your trailer
and ran lines.
I imagine you were drinking a Coke
and rubbed the condensation on it
and said sorry to no one in particular.

I never liked a girl well enough to give her twelve sharp knives.

I like it when you sit on the kitchen countertop and dangle your legs beside the lazy susan and the spice racks full of tiny liquor bottles. You like to use your French in the kitchen. You wear it like a doily apron that doesn't really keep flour off of your shirt.

I like it when you fry chicken. Your hands so thin and small, completely unlike lady fingers. I watch you slap the fat of the skinless thighs with your palms. You roll them over and over in the flour; it's so sexy. You're in there with flour up to your elbows rolling the bird around with your bare hands and every once in a while you roll your shoulders back and turn your head in my direction.

But right now you're making cookies.

You bought one of those logs of cookie dough with the marks that show you where to cut. Some of them are too skinny or too fat. You cover up the mistakes with green and red sprinkles. Those are the best ones. You're kind of singing and doing that thing where you curl your toes and bounce like you're dancing.

I'm sweating under this turtleneck.

All the light is kind of rosy and warm. It could be the wine. Either way, I just want you here where this embroidered pillow is. I want you to rub my receding hairline and call me Lumpy and kiss me like we're standing in the produce aisle.

You're on a gravy train with biscuit wheels.

Q:
A: I had a hand in his loss of the hand, so what?
He got a prosthetic.
He can still stick those stubby wooden nubs
into the marble holes.
What about me?
Nobody can buy back that championship.
Nobody can buy back my hair
and the girls
and the booze
and the title.

Q:
A: I'll tell ya. I've been living in a La Quinta
for the past five years.
Good people.
They keep the towels hot and the tiles cold.
Sometimes I smoke on the balcony
and watch the maids push those carts
from room to room.
Every now and then they knock on my door.
I don't say anything.
I just stand on the balcony
and listen to them pick up my things
and set them down.

Q:
A: Wax, like the kind you use to keep your braces from
cutting your lips.
I just pick it up from the dentist,
tell him my root canal is bothering me.

He gives me a bag of samples,
and I melt them in the microwave.
You have to add some milk to it or whiskey or
something to make it the right consistency.
Then I just stick my hands in and rub my hair down.
It keeps everything in place.
See, I have hair. It's growing, just not
in the right places.

Q:
A: I don't use a ball anymore.
I don't even wear my own shoes.
I've gotten used to that deodorizer
they spray into the soles,
erasing the prints of whatever size 10 ½
came before me.
Get my own lane and set my nachos
and my beer
and my soft pretzel
on the seats beside me.
I make up names for the other people
on the electronic score card.
Sometimes the presidents.

Q:
A: In ten years?
In ten years I hope I don't have
dirty laundry on my floor
and half empties on top of the TV.

The crying on the inside kind, I guess.

The vagaries of a child's birthday party:
a balloon popped under the weight of Osh-Kosh-B'gosh;
a warm puppy licking the top off of an ice cream cone;
a cake smashed in by a tiny fist.

We tally up the list,
take a sip of wine
from party hats
for each tick.

Human decay is not ideal at a joint like this,
so here we are in full clown makeup,
white face and red lips and frown lines,
so you get the idea.

A birthday cake shaped like a miniature poodle
has just been consumed,
each piece a small dismemberment
until that poor pooch was a paraplegic.

Prince said parties weren't meant to last.
I guess he's been to a child's birthday party
where the entertainment,
even Bill Murray in full clown makeup,
can't hold a gaze as long as the family dog
mounting a rather realistic
balloon animal.

I hope you've had enough to drink. It's going to take courage.

The movie began on the back of a balding man's head. I was warm and rosy from fistfuls of airplane Champagne, floating me to the roof of the cabin Wonka's-fizzy-lifting-drink-style.

On the screen, colors wipe across your cab window in streaks of rain. Head on glass, you sleep between turns, consider the chances of the driver reaching your stop and carrying you up to your room the way your parents would when you fell asleep in the back seat. You're looking out the window toward... what? Toward uncertainty?

Yeah, me too. I pull up the plastic shade and look at the wisps of night cloud cotton balls stretched over black poster board held in front of the window to simulate flight and think of my own uncertainty waiting for me with a paper sign that reads "Shea Stripling's uncertainty" at Gate 7.

But I'm buoyed a bit by the booze, lifted with the spirit of spirits, and full of new love, that delicate mask you pull down from the overhead bin and breathe in so so deeply until you're all dizzy with that pure oxygen to the brain.

And then there's the karaoke scene. Fireworks on weather balloons. It's a pink wig girl meets an orange camouflage shirt turned inside-out guy story. You know the kind. I'm more of an ABBA and blonde wig with a bald spot you have to cover with a scarf kind of girl, but I like Roxy Music, and I like your rendition in particular, which is why I push the free earbuds deep into the curly cue holes and sing in a Champagne slur.

And so what if that was my foot in my sock you

were holding? What advice would you impart to me? Does it get easier Bob, or Bill, or whatever you prefer to hear coming out of my mouth in this scene? Is there anything more than sakura blossoms and silence over sake?

No.

Yes.

And then, somehow, we're at the end, and you look out that cab window, and I look out my plastic airplane window.

Hey, you. And you hold the back of my head, stroke my hair, whisper.

Just like honey.

Epilogue

It's as difficult as reconstructing a kiss. I can give you the time of day, the placement of the hands, the location of the sun. But I can't give you the kiss.

I turn the memory over and over in my hands, searching for a watermark. Each time I retrieve it, I find it changed.

Grown rosier.

Grown sweeter.

Grown warmer to the touch.

I purchased a croissant and a coffee in the Paris airport as you do when you make it close enough to press your nose to Paris behind glass, but not close enough to get the free smells.

After a shuffle, I was seated in the middle seat of the middle row on the final flight before home. I sat awake all night trying not to disturb the strangers wrapped in their complimentary blankets. The last bit of *The Razor's Edge* had slipped by quicker than I expected, so I was left with eight hours of sleepless free time. I picked up my fraying copy of *The Razor's Edge* and began skimming through lines I had highlighted, comments I had made in the margins through the course of the trip.

After the breakfasts wrapped in cellophane were passed around, I took a dry shower in the bathroom. The next bit was spent waiting. Waiting for passengers to remove their overhead luggage, waiting for the plane to reach the terminal, waiting for the rest of my party to exit the plane, waiting to have my passport checked. While waiting for said passport to be checked, I noticed a guy wearing a plaid shirt that looked vaguely familiar.

I only caught a short glimpse of his warm and sleepy face before I was shuffled forward in line. It was a face that gave me a dim jolt of recognition, a face I felt I had dreamed.

Now waiting by the luggage carousel, I had to prop myself up on my bag to stave off sleep. I was the first of the marching band party (one piccolo in a mass of marching band musicians returning from an Italian tour) to retrieve my bags, which meant I had more waiting to look forward to until the rest of my party was ready to board the bus back to Tuscaloosa. I stood formulating funny anecdotes about the parade through the streets of Florence, my night spent sipping sparkling wine in a foreign bath tub, when I saw the man in plaid again. He was standing alone by an empty luggage cart. He was familiar. More than familiar. A face like a star you've seen at your window.

"You're Bill, right?"

"Yeah. Who am I talkin' to here?"

I don't know what I looked like at that moment of recognition, but inside I was all Roman candles. Overwhelmed by a feeling I had only experienced while watching the third act of *Lost in Translation*, I somehow compelled myself to speak.

We talked of my trip to Italy and discussed how lovely Rome was. He asked why I was visiting, which led into a discussion of my status as a piccolo player in a marching band, to which he responded, "Oh, I love a marching band." I had seen a video of him conducting Cornell's marching band and asked if he had enjoyed that. "Oh yeah, it was great. I really wish I had played in one. You know, I learned to play a tuba for a role once. They brought in these professionals to teach me because I only had a few weeks to learn, and they said I was a natural. Maybe I'll buy one someday." Even if he wasn't Bill Murray, I wanted to be involved with a tuba hobbyist.

I asked him what he had been up to in Paris, or if

he, like me, had been elsewhere. He, of course, had been at Cannes Film Festival promoting *Moonrise Kingdom* and poking around a few of his old haunts. He pulled the latest issue of *Vogue* out of his worn leather messenger bag and flipped to a spread about Wes Anderson and the film. "There's our boy. He looks good, doesn't he?" In the way a lovesick teen might ask her crush if he liked movies, I asked if he was excited about the film. "Yeah, I really think it's something great. It may be the best he's done."

Around this time, I began to feel as though I might be bothering him. Not because of any sort of social signals he had begun to send, but just by virtue of the fact that we had been talking for nearly ten minutes without interruption. I was shocked by how ordinary the whole situation was. There were no other fans gawking about, no one else trying to vie for his attention. It was simply the two of us having a pleasant conversation by the luggage carousel.

I wanted to get a photo before we parted, but Bill pointed out that you couldn't take any photos before going through the customs checkpoint across the room. He was waiting for a rather large trunk and said I was welcome to keep him company while he waited. What a way to wait.

He noticed my copy of *The Razor's Edge* under my arm. I had purposely decided not to bring it up because I thought it might seem a bit too on the nose, but when I told him what I was reading he seemed delighted. "It's a great book, isn't it?"

We talked about how fabulous the writing was, how it was underappreciated, and I asked if he would like to sign the title page. "What is this, a library book? I can't desecrate a library book. Here." He handed me his bag, which he began to dig through. He pulled out a fat stack of what appeared to be business cards. "This is my favorite restaurant in Paris. I used to go there all the time when I lived there. I went back while I was in town

— it had to be the first time in twenty years — and I stuck my face through the window to see if the cook was in and said 'Bonjour' thinking the guy was probably dead by now, but there he was and he said, 'Bill, is that you?' To which I responded, 'Oui.'"

The card had a small depiction of a brick café with a line of even windows on the front. Café de la Tourelle. He asked me for a pen and wrote *Shea, Drop my name here. Or take me. Bill Murray* on the back. How wonderful.

I looked down at the card in my hand.

"You should know I'm getting college credits while writing about you."

"Is that so?"

"Yeah, isn't that wonderful?"

"Well, in that case, if you ever need to contact me, here."

And he wrote down a number. *The* number. The number was in my very insignificant hand.

At this point, his leather trunks (these really weathered pieces that looked as though they had been sent through a portal from a bygone Bogart era) appeared on the carousel. "Wait right here." And I did. I watched him cross the room to retrieve the most conspicuous pieces of luggage and saw him briefly look in my direction and wave. Swoon.

He returned with bags in tow prepared to sail through customs when I realized I had left my declaration sheet on the plane. I felt a bit panicked and asked him what he thought I should do. "Well, we've got two agents there. Which one do you think looks the nicest, the one on the left or the one on the right?" I picked right, so we walked up to the counter as nonchalantly as possible. Bill handled the whole situation.

"Hey there, how are you? This is Shea, and she's left her customs sheet on the plane. Is it OK if we just walk through anyway?"

"Are you Bill? Bill Murray?"

"Yeah, nice to see ya."

"Is she with you?"

"Well, we've been talking for the last twenty minutes, so I'd say yes."

"Alright, you can come on through."

And we did walk right through to the area of the airport where pictures could be taken. I had only a disposable Kodak with, mercifully, a few shots left to click. Bill snagged a lady who worked at the airport to take our shot. She also thought Bill's face looked a bit familiar.

"You look like a celebrity. Oh, who is it?"

"Eddie Murphy."

She crumpled with laughter, a physical reaction that is always in the vicinity of Bill Murray.

We posed in front of the Atlanta International Airport sign. The first was just a natural shot, his arm around my back. For the second, he suggested we stand back-to-back, which evoked a scene of long lost friends comparing height changes since their last reunion. For the last, he crouched down and said, "I don't know what this is, but let's do this." And so we did.

The camera was back in my hand, and it looked like our brief encounter was coming to a close. He started to walk toward the connecting flights area, so I said, "Well, I guess this is goodbye."

"You're not going to a connecting flight?"

"No, they have a bus for us outside."

"You're taking a bus all the way back to Tuscaloosa? Well."

He pulled me into his arms, hugged me close, and kissed both of my cheeks as I kissed both of his. We started to part, and all I could think to say was "Arrivederci, Bill."

"Arrivederci, Shea."

Thanks

for being the first one to make the move and making everything wonderful thereafter happen: Lynsey Morandin.

for knowing how to best light my face (the good side) and this book: Jeremy Bronaugh.

for laughing at and with me and bringing the wine bottle large enough to share: The Couple Bronaugh.

for continually inviting me back to rooms with microphones and warmth: Kimberly Casey.

for the blueberries and the lighthouse: Crimothy Toft.

for the night of the living diners and disco fries: Katherine Kosich.

for the photo of the elephant at Foodland: Austin Long.

for thinking this was a good idea: Ashley McWaters.

for thinking this was a bad idea: Billy Fields.

for their tenderness and leaving the radio on something nice: my parents